ID650022

READING POWER

Helping Organizations

ASPCA
The American Society for the Prevention of Cruelty to Animals

Anastasia Suen

The Rosen Publishing Group's
PowerKids Press™
New York

Published in 2002 by The Rosen Publishing Group, Inc.
29 East 21st Street, New York, NY 10010

First Edition

Book Design: Michelle Innes

Photo Credits: Cover, pp. 4–7, 14, 16, 19 © ASPCA; pp. 8, 15
© Hulton-Deutsch Collection/Corbis; p. 9 © Picture Press/Corbis;
pp. 10–11 © Bettmann/Corbis; p. 12 © Roger Ressmeyer/Corbis;
p. 13 © AFP/Corbis; p. 17 © Robert Maass/Corbis; p. 21 (top)
© Reflections Photolibrary/Corbis; p. 21 (bottom left) © Philip James Corwin/Corbis;
p. 21 (bottom right) © Paul A. Souders/Corbis

Suen, Anastasia.
The American Society for the Prevention of Cruelty to Animals /
Anastasia Suen.
    p. cm. — (Helping organizations)
Includes bibliographical references and index.
ISBN 0-8239-6004-8 (lib. bdg.)
1. American Society for the Prevention of Cruelty to Animals—Juvenile
literature. 2. Animal welfare—United States—Juvenile literature. [1.
American Society for the Prevention of Cruelty to Animals. 2.
Animals—Treatment.] I. Title.
HV4763 .S84 2001
179'.3'06073—dc21
                                        2001001120

Manufactured in the United States of America

Contents

The Beginning of the ASPCA

Henry Bergh wanted to help animals. He did not like the way some people treated them. In 1866, he began The American Society for the Prevention of Cruelty to Animals.

The ASPCA is the oldest humane organization in the United States.

Henry Bergh

The ASPCA helps animals in many ways. In 1876, the ASPCA began an ambulance service for horses. The ambulance service helped horses that were hurt.

It's a Fact

The first ambulance service for people did not begin until 1878.

Henry Bergh also invented a sling to lift horses that fell into rivers or got stuck in mud.

ASPCA Classes

In 1916, the ASPCA began having classes for children. The classes taught children how to look after animals. The ASPCA has taught many children across the United States how to take care of their pets.

The ASPCA has classes for animals, too. These classes are called obedience classes. In obedience classes, dogs are taught how to do things like sit, stay, or come when called.

The first ASPCA obedience classes began in 1944.

Finding Homes

The ASPCA has a shelter for animals in New York City. The shelter finds homes for many animals. In 1998, the ASPCA helped to find good homes for 1,250 animals.

The ASPCA and more than 200 other groups help greyhounds find new homes after they stop racing.

Greyhounds Adopted Across the Country

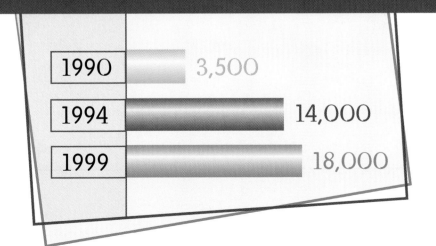

1990	3,500
1994	14,000
1999	18,000

Sometimes animals in the shelter are not ready to go to new homes. They may be sick or hurt. People help to care for these animals for a short time. When the animals feel better, the ASPCA finds good homes for them.

A Hospital for Animals

The ASPCA also has a hospital for animals in New York City. The ASPCA's hospital helps about 30,000 animals each year.

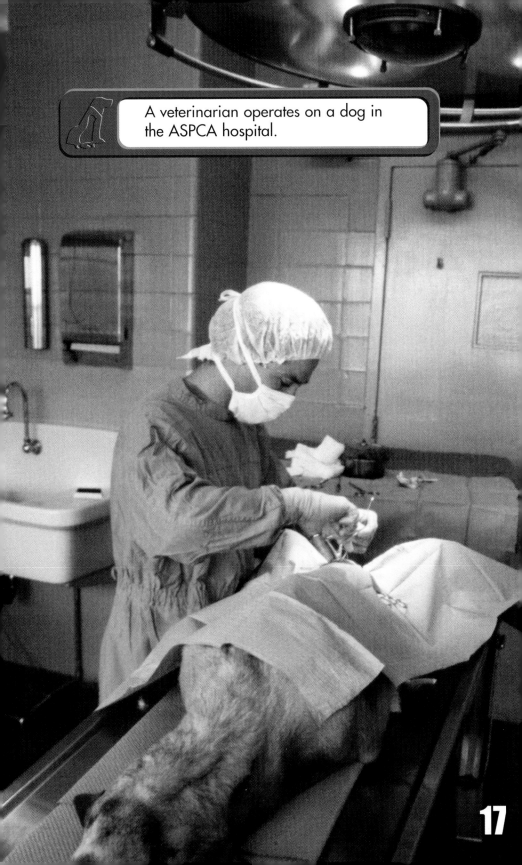

A veterinarian operates on a dog in the ASPCA hospital.

Keeping Animals Healthy

Sometimes animals eat things that make them sick. The ASPCA helps those animals, too. Pet owners across the United States can call for help if they have an emergency.

It's a Fact

In 2000, the ASPCA answered 60,000 calls for help or information.

This ASPCA worker helps people when they call for information.

Today, dogs, cats, and other animals are living longer, happier lives than ever before. The ASPCA works hard to make sure animals across the United States are safe and healthy.

21

Glossary

ambulance (**am**-byuh-luhns) a vehicle that carries sick or injured animals or people

cruelty (**kroo**-uhl-tee) pain or suffering caused by others

emergency (ih-**mer**-juhn-see) a time when help is needed fast

humane (hyoo-**mayn**) kind

obedience (oh-**bee**-dee-uhns) when you do what you are told to do

prevention (prih-**vehn**-shuhn) keeping something from happening

shelter (**shehl**-tuhr) a building where animals without homes may live

veterinarian (**vet**-uhr-uh-**nehr**-ee-uhn) a doctor who treats animals

Resources

Books

ASPCA Pet Care Guides for Kids: Kitten
by Mark Evans
DK Publishing, Inc. (1992)

ASPCA Pet Care Guides for Kids: Puppy
by Mark Evans
DK Publishing, Inc. (1992)

Web Site

ASPCA Animaland
http://www.animaland.org/index.asp

Index

Word Count: 294

Note to Librarians, Teachers, and Parents

If reading is a challenge, Reading Power is a solution! Reading Power is perfect for readers who want high-interest subject matter at an accessible reading level. These fact-filled, photo-illustrated books are designed for readers who want straightforward vocabulary, engaging topics, and a manageable reading experience. With clear picture/text correspondence, leveled Reading Power books put the reader in charge. Now readers have the power to get the information they want and the skills they need in a user-friendly format.